TRADITIONS AND CELEBRATIONS

EASTER

by Nicole A. Mansfield

PEBBLE
a capstone imprint

Published by Pebble, an imprint of Capstone
1710 Roe Crest Drive, North Mankato, Minnesota 56003
capstonepub.com

Copyright © 2024 by Capstone. All rights reserved. No part of this publication may be reproduced in whole or in part, or stored in a retrieval system, or transmitted in any form or by any means, electronic, mechanical, photocopying, recording, or otherwise, without written permission of the publisher.

Library of Congress Cataloging-in-Publication Data is available on the Library of Congress website.

ISBN: 9780756576912 (hardcover)
ISBN: 9780756577032 (paperback)
ISBN: 9780756577049 (ebook PDF)

Summary: Easter is a Christian holiday that celebrates Jesus Christ dying and coming back to life. People attend church. They also gather for a big meal and activities like egg hunts. Discover how people around the world celebrate this holiday.

Editorial Credits
Editor: Ericka Smith; Designer: Kayla Rossow; Media Researcher: Svetlana Zhurkin; Production Specialist: Katy LaVigne

Image Credits
Alamy: Ian Lamond, 12; Dreamstime: Pgibowicz, 29; Getty Images: Amir Levy, 11, Anadolu Agency/Jacek Boczarski, 5, Franco Origlia, 21, Fred de Noyelle, 13, Jose Luis Pelaez Inc, 18, SolStock, 9, The Denver Post/MediaNews Group/Helen H. Richardson, 8; National Park Service: Anthony DeYoung, 19; Newscom: Toby Adamson, 22; Shutterstock: andia, 17, AS Foodstudio, 23, Byron Ortiz, 27, Catalin Rusnac, 16, Elena Veselova, 15, Jag_cz, cover, Lucy.Brown, 28, oliveromg, 7, praszkiewicz, 25, Rafal Kulik (background), back cover and throughout, Roman Samborskyi, 1

All internet sites appearing in back matter were available and accurate when this book was sent to press.

TABLE OF CONTENTS

WHAT IS EASTER?... 4

WHEN IS EASTER? 6

WHO CELEBRATES EASTER?..................... 8

HOW DO PEOPLE CELEBRATE
EASTER? 10

EASTER TRADITIONS AROUND
THE WORLD... 18

    GLOSSARY... 30

    READ MORE 31

    INTERNET SITES 31

    INDEX 32

    ABOUT THE AUTHOR 32

Words in **bold** are in the glossary.

WHAT IS EASTER?

Wooden crosses are draped with white fabric. Families wear their nicest clothes. People go to church. It is Easter!

Easter is a Christian holiday. Christians are followers of Jesus Christ. Their holy book is called the Bible. The Bible teaches that Jesus died to save the world from **sin**. Then, on the third day after his death, he came back to life.

On Easter, Christians celebrate Jesus coming back to life—his **resurrection**.

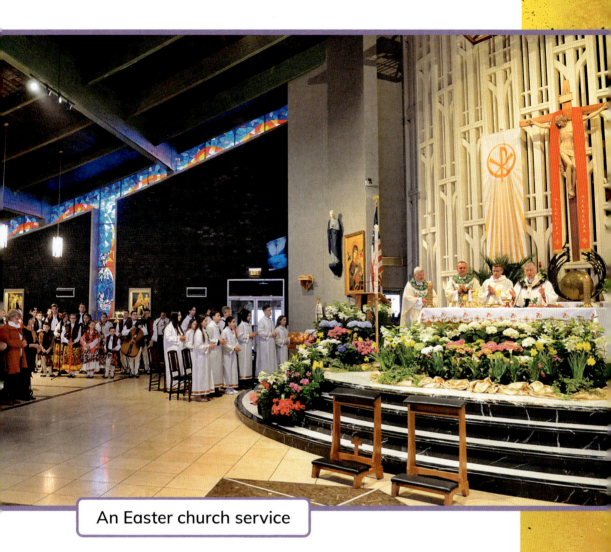

An Easter church service

WHEN IS EASTER?

Easter is on a Sunday in March or April. The date changes each year. But it is always the first Sunday after the **vernal equinox**. The vernal equinox marks the beginning of spring.

WHO CELEBRATES EASTER?

Christians celebrate Easter all around the world! In the United States, about 80 percent of people celebrate Easter. In the last hundred years, many non-Christians have started to celebrate Easter too.

HOW DO PEOPLE CELEBRATE EASTER?

LENT & GOOD FRIDAY

Many Christians prepare for Easter during Lent. Lent begins 40 days before Easter Sunday. During Lent, people **fast**. They don't eat certain foods, like meat, or at certain times. They might give up favorite foods or activities too.

Good Friday is the Friday before Easter. It is the day Jesus died. Some Christians go to church on Good Friday. Some people fast too.

People celebrating Good Friday in Jerusalem, Israel

EASTER SUNDAY SERVICE

Finally, on Easter Sunday, Christians usually attend a service at church or outdoors. Some Christians go to church before sunrise. They watch the sun come up. It reminds them that Jesus rose after his death.

Jesus Christ rising from the dead

EASTER MEALS

Traditional Easter meals are a part of the celebration. Meals have meat like ham or chicken, vegetables, potatoes, and bread. Since many Christians fast before Easter, a large meal is a welcome way to celebrate.

EASTER EGGS

Early Christians did not eat eggs during the week before Easter. But their chickens still laid eggs! People started gathering the eggs and decorating them instead. They called them Holy Week eggs. Now, eggs are a common symbol of Easter.

The baby chickens that hatch from eggs have become a symbol of Easter too. On Easter, Jesus came out of his grave. Both represent new life.

EASTER TRADITIONS AROUND THE WORLD

UNITED STATES

Many Americans dye eggs for Easter. Usually, they use bright spring colors! Some people add stickers or patterns to their Easter eggs.

The Easter Egg Roll at the White House

Easter egg hunts are really popular in the United States. Adults hide Easter eggs in their yards. Then kids have fun searching for the eggs. Some churches host huge Easter egg hunts for their community.

There is also an Easter Egg Roll each year at the White House in Washington, DC. The big event takes place on the Monday after Easter. In 2023, about 30,000 people participated!

ITALY

In Italy, thousands of people go to Vatican City on Easter. They come from all around the world. They want to listen to the Pope's Easter blessing. The Pope is an important Christian leader. He is the head of the Catholic Church. Catholics are one of many types of Christians. Every Easter the Pope gives a blessing from a church balcony.

People listening to the Pope's Easter blessing

ETHIOPIA

Ethiopians have a much longer period of fasting before Easter than Christians in other places. For about 55 days, they give up meat and dairy products.

On the Saturday before Easter, churches hold **vigils**. Then, there's a service that lasts until three o'clock in the morning on Easter. They have a small meal and then rest.

Doro wat

Later in the day, they have a big feast. Most people eat a traditional food called *doro wat*, a chicken stew.

POLAND

People in Poland get wet to celebrate Easter! The boys start a fun water fight against the girls. The surprise soaking starts the Monday after Easter. They may use water guns, water balloons, or buckets for the water fight. The next day, it's the girls' turn to **drench** the boys.

Some believe this tradition started to celebrate rain. The spring rain made new crops grow. Easter also happens in spring. It celebrates new life.

GUATEMALA

On Easter the streets of Guatemala are filled with color! Artists create beautiful designs on the ground. Their designs tell the story of Jesus's life, death, and resurrection. These designs are called *alfombras*.

People use fruits, flowers, and dyed sawdust to fill in the designs. It looks like a colorful carpet on the street. Some of the designs can be up to a half-mile long!

Alfombras are a symbol of the beauty of Christ's path. Jesus walked to the cross to die for people's sins on the Friday before Easter. On Good Friday the townspeople walk on the alfombras toward their church.

People in Honduras and El Salvador create alfombras too.

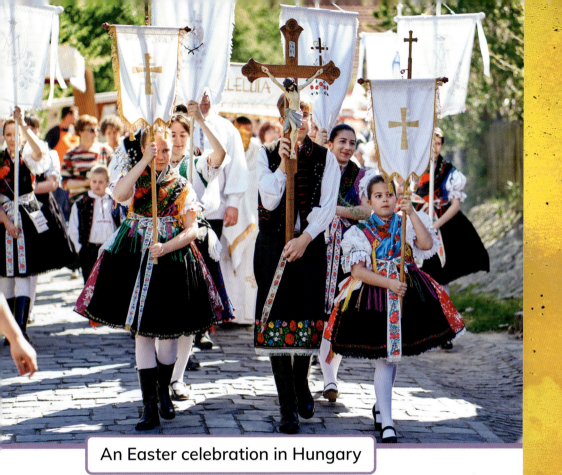

An Easter celebration in Hungary

The Easter season is an important time for worship, community, and celebration for Christians. All around the world, Christians have created traditions to honor Jesus Christ's death and resurrection.

GLOSSARY

drench (DRENCH)—to make completely wet

fast (FAST)—to give up eating for a period of time for religious reasons

resurrection (rez-uh-REK-shun)—rising from the dead

sin (SIN)—an act that goes against religious rules

vernal equinox (VUR-nuhl EE-kwuh-noks)—the moment when the sun crosses the equator, marking the start of spring in the northern hemisphere

vigil (VIJ-uhl)—a period of time spent doing something through the night, like watching, guarding, or praying

READ MORE

Amstutz, Lisa J. *Wesak*. North Mankato, MN: Capstone, 2024.

Raij, Emily. *Christmas*. North Mankato, MN: Capstone, 2022.

Salu, Sharon Abimbola. *Easter in Lagos*. Self-published, 2020.

INTERNET SITES

Britannica Kids: Easter
kids.britannica.com/kids/article/Easter/353077

Kiddle: Easter Facts for Kids
kids.kiddle.co/Easter

National Geographic Kids: Spring Celebrations
kids.nationalgeographic.com/celebrations/article/spring-celebrations

INDEX

doro wat, 23

Easter eggs, 16–17, 18–19

El Salvador, 28

Ethiopia, 22–23

Good Friday, 10, 11, 28

Guatemala, 26–28

Honduras, 28

Hungary, 29

Italy, 20–21

Jerusalem, Israel, 11

Lent, 10

Poland, 24–25

Pope, 20, 21

resurrection, 4, 12, 13, 26, 29

United States, 8, 18–19

Vatican City, 20

vernal equinox, 6

vigils, 22

Washington, DC, 19

White House, 19

ABOUT THE AUTHOR

Nicole A. Mansfield is a mother to her "sweet three" and is married to an Air Force officer. Nicole and her family are Christians. Easter has always been her favorite holiday! Writing this book that tells what Easter is all about is a highlight of Nicole's writing career! Nicole's special interests include singing on her worship team at church and serving in the children's ministry.